D1391364

OUR BRITISH BIRDS

OUR BRITISH BIRDS

SPOTTING AND JOTTING GUIDE

MATT SEWELL

EBURY
PRESS

1 3 5 7 9 10 8 6 4 2

Ebury Press, an imprint of Ebury Publishing,
20 Vauxhall Bridge Road,
London SW1V 2SA

Penguin
Random House
UK

Ebury Press is part of the Penguin Random House group
of companies whose addresses can be found at
global.penguinrandomhouse.com

Artworks have appeared in Matt Sewell's previous books:
Our Garden Birds (2012), *Our Songbirds* (2013), *Our
Woodland Birds* (2014) and *Owls* (2014) with the exception
of those on pages 73, 74, 75, 76, 77, 78 and 92.

www.eburypublishing.co.uk

A CIP catalogue record for this book is available from the
British Library

ISBN 9780091960001

Penguin Random House is committed to a sustainable future
for our business, our readers and our planet. This book is
made from Forest Stewardship Council® certified paper.

MIX
Paper from
responsible sources
FSC® C104723

To my Goldfinches – Jess, Romy and Mae

CONTENTS

'Everyone likes birds. What wild
creature is more accessible to our eyes
and ears, as close to us and everyone
in the world, as universal as a bird?'

David Attenborough

INTRODUCTION

It's easy to go bird spotting, you don't even need to leave your house or to have finished your breakfast to do it, as those few metres outside your window hold just as many spotting and jotting opportunities as there are up in the wood or down in the estuary. Even walking to work/school/the pub can be a golden chance for getting that triumphant first spot and elusive tick. All you need to do is be aware and look at every bird that passes by. Yes, every bird! That Pigeon could easily be a Sparrow Hawk, that Sea Gull a Buzzard or that Blue Tit a Firecrest (although I am always happy to see a Blue Tit!). So go on, get outside, get spotting and jotting and see how many ticks you can get. And remember to always look up!

BIRDS

☐ Goldfinch
Carduelis carduelis

There's nothing more delightful than
a charm of Goldfinches, chiming from
thistle to branch.

☐ Greenfinch
Carduelis chloris

Not as green or pretty as you would imagine, but a lovely bird nonetheless.

🔲 Chaffinch
Fringilla coelebs

Very pretty but common as muck: they loiter
at beauty spots scrounging for crisp crumbs.

☑ Bullfinch
Pyrrhula pyrrhula

An enchanting bird: playful yet shy, petite and possessing a pink and black coat of graphic perfection.

☐ House Sparrow
Passer domesticus

As British as chip butties, looking like an old
RAF Squadron Leader in a flat cap and tweed.

☐ The Nuthatch and the Treecreeper
Sitta europaea and *Certhia familiaris*

Committed forest dwellers, these guys not only fly but their second nature is to walk wherever they want to.

☑ Blue Tit
Cyanistes caeruleus

Bramble-pickers. These Tits gorge themselves, plop out the seeds the other end and help the thorny bushes spread.

☑ Great Tit
Parus major

Most handsome and bossiest of the
tits, mainly found letting everyone know the
news with one of his many loud songs.

☐ Long-tailed Tit
Aegithalos caudatus

A rather unfortunately
named little bundle of joy.
Tiny clouds in tracksuits.
I love them.

☐ Firecrest and Goldcrest
Regulus ignicapillus and
Regulus regulus

Smallest birds in Britain: they weigh
roughly the same as a teaspoonful of sugar
or a mouthful of air.

☐ Bearded Tit
Panarus biarmicus

An absolute beauty of a bird: striking eyewear, pastel tones and long, luxurious tail feathers.

☐ Wheatear
Oenanthe oenanthe

A Wheatear keeps his distance, but try to catch a glimpse of his splendid blue gilet.

☐ Linnet
Carduelis cannabina

Slight and endearing, the Linnet is often found in dense spiky hedgerows. Cute as your first crush.

☐ Yellowhammer
Emberiza citrinella

A jittery jibber-jabber who keeps the
hillside updated about the slightest details
with his nervy, high-pitched chatter.

☐ Cirl Bunting
Emberiza cirlus

Sage green, butter yellow and earthy
ochre, this rare beauty is confined
to pockets of coastal Devon.

☐ Song Thrush
Turdus philomelos

A songbird professional that belts out every number like it's the finale to a grand show.

☐ Redwing
Turdus iliacus

Looks like a thrush that mistook a can of red spray-paint for deodorant and headed out for the day.

☑ Blackbird
Turdus merula

Heaven forbid you stand within ten metres
of a Blackbird's nest: Britain's most common
bird will meet you eyeball to eyeball.

☐ Ring Ouzel
Turdus torquatus

Despite being most commonly spotted on scrubby hillsides, this dapper Blackbird's brother sports a dinner jacket.

☑ Robin
Erithacus rubecula

Not just for Christmas: whether a golden
oldie or a carol, the Robin sings his song all
year round.

☐ Nightingale
Luscinia megarhynchos

However far into the hedgerow this shy
songbird hides himself, his luminous song
will be glorified in folklore.

☐ Redstart
Phoenicurus phoenicurus

One of the most dashingly handsome of
the garden visitors, he just darts about
flashing his beautiful orange tail.

☐ Garden Warbler
Sylvia borin

A diamond in the rough, this diminutive songbird's hidden talent for singing is a closely guarded secret.

☐ Wood Warbler
Phylloscopus sibilatrix

Listen to a warbler and you'll discover that
each is an individual, with rattles, languid
songs, whistles and chiffchaffings.

☐ Dartford Warbler
Sylvia undata

A regular visitor from southern Europe.
Like a singing thistle in a bobble hat.

☐ Blackcap
Sylvia atricapilla

A sleek, handsome bird; maybe not a
warbler by name, but he is so in form,
function and voice.

☐ Wren
Troglodytes troglodytes

A tiny, busy, hardy bird that won't mind
telling anybody to sling their hook.

Dipper
Cinclus cinclus

This songbird prefers feeding underwater,
bobbing about whilst reciting his
immaculate crystal-clear song.

☐ Waxwing
Bombycilla garrulus

Like a computer-generated samurai finch
designed by a Norse god. Who knows what
a Waxwing is capable of.

☐ Ring-necked Parakeet
Psittacula krameri

Although sometimes bullies, Parakeets
bring groovy colours and far-out vibes
to London's outside spaces.

☑ Crow
Corvus corone

Followed by malice, fear and omens, the
Crow's tough black exterior covers an even
darker menace lingering inside.

☐ Rook
Corvus frugilegus

With a clownish face and dishevelled
appearance, these croakers aren't out to cause
mischief like their cousins, the Crow.

☑ Jackdaw
Corvus monedula

One of the only birds to have white irises, the
Jackdaw is never afraid to hold your gaze.

☐ Magpie
Pica pica

With a call like dial-up internet and an oil-slick black coat, this crow is a bird of ill omen.

☐ Jay
Garrulus glandarius

One of the moustachioed Jay's favourite
foods is the mighty acorn, which he
frantically collects and hides for a later day.

☐ Raven
Corvus corax

Rolling his 'r's like a yokel, the Raven loves to mouth off with his trademark guttural command: the 'kronk'.

☐ Chough

Pyrrhocorax pyrrhocorax

You can be nothing but chuffed if you spot
one of these fine West Coast beauties.

☐ Starling
Sturnus vulgaris

This scraggly unsociable gang member is actually a gifted songbird – thanks to the wizardry of mimicry.

☐ Great Grey Shrike
Lanius excubitor

Perched up high, surveying his plot before swiping his prey, this wannabe raptor wears a mask to conceal his identity.

☐ Pied Wagtail
Motacilla alba

This bird is always on the go, bouncing
around to catch the tiniest of flies, with
utter joy and ease.

☑ Skylark
Alauda arvensis

Flying high, singing crystalline
enchantments before parachuting down,
the Skylark rises and breaks hearts.

☐ Kingfisher
Alcedo atthis

A celestial work of art. The Kingfisher offers just millisecond glimpses before he's off to blow the next yawning mind.

☐ Green Woodpecker
Picus viridis

Outside his camouflage of leaves, this guy's
a neon powerball bouncing through the
thicket, flying like a madman.

☑ Great Spotted Woodpecker
Dendrocopos major

Less of a try-hard than the Green
Woodpecker, this fellow keeps himself
to himself.

☐ Lesser Spotted Woodpecker
Dendrocopos minor

Half the size of the Great Woodpecker, but every bit as beautiful with its dazzling monochrome climbingwear and red beret.

☐ Wryneck
Jynx torquilla

In their defence, these little birds writhe
their necks to disturbing angles and hiss
like snakes – hence the name.

☐ Swallow
Hirundo rustica

Like an old friend
returning for the summer,
filling the room with
laughter, then disappearing
before you know it.

58

☐ House Martin
Delichon urbica

These friendly birds spend their days frolicking mid-flight, making flying look like the fun we know it would be.

☐ Swift

Apus apus

Like a bow that took flight with the arrow,
it is claimed the Swift spends more time in
the air than any other bird.

☐ Nightjar
Caprimulgus europaeus

With nocturnal habits, big eyes and an even bigger mouth, the Nightjar has mystified the human race for centuries.

☑ Barn Owl
Tyto alba

Symbolism has given owls bad press,
but in truth the Barn Owl is magical and
otherworldly, shimmering like a royal ghost.

☑ Tawny Owl
Strix aluco

Perhaps the wisest-looking owl, and
huggable too until you see those talons and
the fearsome beak behind the fluff.

☐ Long-eared Owl
Asio otus

The Long-eared Owl, arrogant and vain,
with every right to be. What a dish!

☐ Short-eared Owl
Asio flammeus

Like she has been caught in the sunny daytime after she has been up all night, she has a face like thunder. Don't get in her way; she needs her kip.

☐ Little Owl
Athene noctua

This tranquil fellow can be found in
daylight. Bid him 'Good day' and he will
nod back in respect.

☐ Cuckoo
Cuculus canorus

Her self-aggrandising song is as infamous as her dubious parenting, but the Cuckoo is vital to our landscape.

☑ Wood Pigeon
Columba palumbus

Like a half-cut granddad, proud as punch
at his granddaughter's wedding, stuffed to
the gunnels with food and booze.

☐ Collared Dove
Streptopelia decaocto

A polite bird that has colonised almost
everywhere between here and his humble
beginnings in India.

☐ Turtle Dove
Streptopelia turtur

A glamorous granny resplendent in lace and
pastel knickerbockers. Increasingly rare –
they don't make them like that anymore.

☑ Great Black-backed Gull
Larus marinus

Top of the food chain; as big as an
Alsatian; nothing is off the menu for
nature's cruel messenger.

☐ Herring Gull
Larus argentatus

Disturber of peace, raider of bins, mugger of vinegary chips and sound of a thousand seaside memories.

☐ Guillemot
Uria aalge

One of the most common coastal birds
remains a lucky spot: the Guillemot lives
out of reach atop white cliffs.

☐ Puffin
Fratercula arctica

Like face-painted puppies at a seaside
birthday party, off their faces on sugar and
E-numbers!

☐ Gannet
Morus bassanus

Sleek and aerodynamic like an Olympic
time-trial cyclist, but with a bad reputation
for being a greedy guts.

☐ Cormorant
Phalacrocorax carbo

The fisherman's nemesis, this coastal
bird moves upstream during the
summer for pescetarian banquets and
scares the anglers away.

☑ Mallard

Anas platyrhynchos

These ducks are known for their fondness
for white bread crusts and for having a
harsh way with the ladies.

☐ Smew

Mergus albellus

My favourite duck and he also very helpfully
has my favourite bird's name too. He's ace!

☐ Lapwing
Vanellus vanellus

A once common voice. So common that many know this handsome plover by his call alone: the 'peewit'.

☐ Avocet
Recurvirostra avosetta

Striking and elegant, the Avocet belongs on catwalks in Paris rather than boggy coastal sanctuaries in Suffolk.

☑ Oystercatcher
Haematopus ostralegus

A sturdy, handsome coastal bird that sings
(or shouts, to be honest) his heart out to
lure the ladies.

☐ Bittern
Botaurus stellaris

Deep in the marshlands dwells the Bittern:
part myth, part Heron. Attracts a lady with
his guttural sonic 'boom'.

☐ Coot
Fulica atra

Like a Moorhen wearing a swimming cap,
the Coot is not known for his call but
you'd recognise the loud honk.

☐ Moorhen
Gallinula chloropus

The Moorhen is in fact found everywhere
from parks to ponds – not up on the moors.

☐ Canada Goose
Branta canadensis

You can't beat the sight of these friendly
fowl in flight, spread in a V formation,
honking their heads off.

🗒 Woodcock
Scolopax rusticola

You'll hear him coming: 'Fart, fart, peep!'
This little set of bagpipes is considered a
delicacy and is hunted in some parts.

Pheasant

Phasianus colchicus

Bottle green and golden chestnut, with a
tail that streaks like a comet, the Pheasant
is a work of celestial beauty.

☐ Red Kite
Milvus milvus

These massive raptors cheer up many a journey along certain motorways of the British Isles.

☑ Buzzard
Buteo buteo

Our tiny eagle, blonde and compact, can be found soaring high above farmlands and rolling hills.

☑ Sparrowhawk
Accipiter nisus

Twice the male's size, the female
Sparrowhawk is the fiercest hunter in the
woods: any bird is a sitting duck.

☐ Golden Eagle
Aquila chrysaetos

Rugged and heroic, spiralling over the
Highlands with a wingspan of two metres,
this Eagle needs no introduction.

☑ Osprey
Pandion haliaetus

Our dexterous sea hawk can plunge deep
to hook his catch or pluck a river salmon
from the air.

☐ Kestrel
Falco tinnunculus

Beautiful, feline birds of prey: the female
is spotty like a flying leopard, the male
handsome in his medieval finery.

☐ Hobby
Falco subbuteo

Resembling a stowaway admiral, the
Hobby's gentlemanly navy blue is
contradicted delightfully with a pair of
scraggy red surf shorts.

☐ Peregrine Falcon
Falco peregrinus

This majestic blue-grey falcon is the
only sentient being that can break the
sound barrier.

ACKNOWLEDGEMENTS

Thank yous:

The Goldfinches, The Sewells, The Lees and The Roses.

Simon, Nicki and everybody at Caught by the River/Heavenly and Ebury Press.

Biggest thanks go to my Mam and Dad for giving me the opportunity to have the kind of feral, outdoor childhood that creates the awe in nature that has fed every page of my books.

My Mam for kindling every creative inspiration I had and for my Dad enthusiastically pointing out every bird he saw and naming it wrongly. He is blind in one eye so we can let that slip – but that passion rubs off.

And lastly to my home patch in Willington, Co. Durham – the Top Dene and The Heap. These are the places where I really learnt to open my eyes. There is wonderment all around us, we just have to allow ourselves to see it.